A Word from the Author

God wants us to worship Him and praise Him for His goodness. That's easy. God is good all the time. It's harder to praise him for the bad things that happen in our lives, for the challenges we face and for the disappointments and difficulties that we have to overcome.

Crazy Praises is my third book of Christian poetry and it invites you to look beyond your troubles and see that God has a way for you. He makes a way when there is no way. He will never give you more than you can bear and we become better for the lessons in life He teaches.

The themes are drawn from everyday living and each one has a prompt that ask why? Then a poem that answers that question.

My prayer is that this book will help you open your mind and renew your faith believing at all times that God has a great plan for your life.

Christine J Bourne

My prayer for all the readers of this book
is that you will see God in a way
you've not seen Him before
A relevant God
A present God
As a living God
Who lives in us and helps us
Change ourselves
Change our lives
Change our world
For the better

Romans 8:28

*"And we know that all things work
together for good to them that love God, to them who
are called according to His purpose"*

King James Version (KJV)

Contents

Our God is a God of everything. He knows everything. He can do everything. He is everything. He is nowhere to be seen but everywhere to be found if we open our eyes and ears, hearts and minds we will see Him, without seeing Him. Is that crazy? Or does it make sense? God promises that He will always be with us.

As we make our way through life, we will see Him manifested as love, as healing, as friendship, as teacher, guide, leader and protector. We will see Him as the helping hand that appears from nowhere when we are in desperate times and don't know what to do.

Through good times and bad, He is ALWAYS with us, unseen but present and it doesn't end there. At the end of our lives, He promises eternal life with Him, to those who believe and follow His ways. From birth to death to eternity, if we commit ourselves to Him, He will protect, provide and prosper us all our days. I praise Him every day for the many ways He has intervened, guided and blessed me.

When I started writing this book, I thought a good way to start would be to make a list of all the things I could praise Him for. It started out small but as I thought back on my life and how God has helped me, the list just got bigger and bigger. He is a wonderful God!

If you can, try to think of times in your life when God has touched your life and praise Him, praise Him, praise Him.

"Praise the Lord, my soul.
I will praise the Lord all my life; I will sing praise to my God as long as I live"

Psalm 146: 1-2
(NIV)

Praise God for Everything

I praise Him and Thank Him for His:

*A*wesomeness, Abundance and Acceptance, Answering prayers and being our Anchor in life's storms

—◆◆◆◆—

*B*lessings and Bible, Beauty and Benevolence, Bearing our sins and for being our Bread of Life through Jesus Christ

—◆◆◆◆—

*C*haracter and Care, Christian Churches, Covenants and for being the great Creator who made heaven and earth and all that is in it

—◆◆◆◆—

*D*ivine Design, Direction, Discipline and Disciples who spread the good news of Jesus Christ, established the church so that 2000 years later, we can praise, worship, love and follow His Ways

—◆◆◆◆—

*E*nergy and Enlightenment, promise of Eternal life to believers and for being our Everpresent help in times of trouble

—◆◆◆◆—

*F*orgiveness and Forgetfulness of our sins, Faithfulness and for being our heavenly Father

—◆◆◆◆—

*G*race and Goodness, Greatness and Grandeur, our Good shepherd and for being the Gate through Jesus Christ

—◆◆◆◆—

*H*ope and Help and Healing, Holy Spirit that lives within us

---

*I*nspiration and Interventions, Intimacy – he knows each of us by name, knows our thoughts and what's in our hearts, Invincibility – there is none that can prevail against Him

---

*J*ustice, Judgement and being our Joy and Justification

---

*K*ingdom to come, Knowledge about all things, being our King

---

*L*ove and Leadership and Law, being the Light of our world, the Living water

---

*M*ercy and Miracles, Majesty and Might, Magnificence

---

*N*udges and Newness of life, No beginning or end

---

*O*pen arms and Omnipotence

---

*P*eace and Perfection, Protection and Provision, Promises and Power, Presence and Purpose and Plans for our lives, Parables by which Jesus taught those who did not know Him

---

*Q*uickness to forgive, being our Quiet place, our Quintessential God – there is none like Him

———◆———

*R*est and Redemption, Reconciliation and Relationship, being Relevant and Real, our Rock and Refuge, our Role Model in Jesus

———◆———

*S*trength we can lean on, Scripture we can rely on, being our Saviour and our Shield

———◆———

*T*ruth and Teaching, Ten Commandments, Trials and Tests by which we grow, if we learn to humble ourselves and rely on God, Trust in Him and His promises

———◆———

*U*nchangeable nature, Unblemished character, Understanding, Unconditional and Unbreakable love, Unfathomable His thoughts, Unequalled His power, Unceasing His care for us

———◆———

*V*ision, Vindication, Victory, Very special love for us

———◆———

*W*isdom and Way, Watchfulness over us, being a Waymaker, miracle Worker, Warrior King, being Worthy of all praise

———◆———

X-traordinary dimension, X-pressiveness in the way He reveals Himself to us through the beauty of nature, the hand of a friend, the trust of an innocent child, the love that we share, the compassion of people who care. God is everywhere – if we look with eyes and hearts open, we will see Him

---

YHWH being Yarweh – the Hebrew word as an expression of God – I AM and absolutely, He is

---

Zeal for us, Zero tolerance for our sins and establishing Zion - Jerusalem in the Holy Land

Prayer

*Thank you, God for everything you have done in my life, for being
a perfect father, teacher, counsellor, protector and provider.*

I am blessed by your love.

You are a mighty God and I worship you and praise you

*May I live each day according to Your Word,
in alignment with Your will and in a way that pleases You*

Amen

Some people might call me crazy about the Bible but I love it! And I praise God for it. It is a book written by men, inspired by God.

The Bible is much more than just words and stories. It is poetry, drama, songs, parables, history lessons and God's love story about us. It is triumphant and transformative.

I read the Bible every day. At first I thought it was a teaching manual on how to live a good and better life and there was a lot I didn't understand. But with each reading and reading different translations, I have gone much deeper to discover the profound truths about human behaviour, the Father's love and how God works in our lives. There are so many AHA! moments and as each new truth is revealed, or assurance given, it makes me excited to see what else I can find. I'm like a treasure hunter, digging for precious pearls of wisdom or solid gold promises of forgiveness, peace and joy.

The Bible is a builder of faith, an illumination of God's character and confirmation that human nature has not changed – at all – over two thousand years. No wonder He gets frustrated with us. No wonder He is overjoyed when we turn from sinful ways and follow Him.

If we take on board the lessons and follow his ways then:

> *"therefore my heart is glad and my spirit rejoices;*
> *my body also will rest secure, because you will not abandon me to*
> *the realm of the dead, nor will you let your faithful one see decay.*
> *You make known to me the path of life; you fill me with joy in*
> *your presence, with eternal pleasures at your right hand"*

Psalm 16:9-11
(NIV)

More than Just a Book

God's Holy Book, the Bible, is an amazing book
Each reading takes you deeper, every time you look
It's a compilation of letters, stories, poems and visions
Songs of praise and of sorrow, forgiveness and of wisdom

It tells the story of creation, of how we came to be
How sin was cast upon us, by the disobedience of Eve
In the beginning there was nothing and from nothing God began
To create the world and all that's in it, then He created Adam

He looked at His work and was very pleased, He planned to live with them in Eden
Then Satan the snake, tempted Eve and now our God is hidden
That simple act of choosing self over God, condemned the world to sin
Through the Bible we see how God loves and wants us, to turn again to Him

The Bible is full of dramatic tales, of people lost and saved
Of Noah's Ark, Jonah's whale and how young David was so brave
It tells of mighty battles when God won for them the victory
And it tells the amazing story of the parting of the Red Sea

It is powerful and compelling as each gripping tale unfolds
Of mankind's state of brokenness and how God's love can grow cold
There are stories of repentance and redemption where God and his people reconcile
And there's plenty of happy endings, but only for a while

For human nature is weak, people think they know it all
When times are good, they move away from God and that leads them to a fall
When times are bad, they get angry and blame God for their troubles
They soon forget that He is God and can help them through their struggles

God chose the Jewish nation to be an example and lead the world away from sin
His plan was for them to follow His Ways, to worship and trust in Him
God wrote the Ten Commandments as laws, to be pleasing in His sight
But human nature is prideful and rebellious, they couldn't see His way was right

He released them from the bondage, of slavery under Pharoah's hand
But their eleven-day trip took forty years, to reach the promised land

In those days there were mighty Kings and warriors who ruled the Jewish nation
The Old Testament tells of many times when God saved their situation

God came up with the ultimate plan, that offered redemption and salvation
One final act of sacrifice to save mankind and lead us from temptation
He sent His son, Jesus Christ, who walked upon the earth
Born of Mary and the Holy Spirit, His was a humble birth

The New Testament starts when Christ appeared, prophesised 700 years before
He is a God of love, of healing and forgiveness, miracles and so much more
The Bible stories are told in parables each one relevant to this day
In the Bible there is so much wisdom, teaching us a better way

Christ suffered and died a horrible death but He did what He was destined to do
To create a new covenant for all, the Gentile and the Jew
A fresh start, new hope and the promise of eternal life
He promised to come again in glory, when the time is right

His active ministry was three short years, but his impact has lasted long
For two thousand years we worship His name and praise him with our songs
The Bible is not just a book, it is a teaching manual for life
Its truths will lead us to peace and joy and doing what is right

We look at our world today and see that human nature remains unchanged
The traps and snares are still waiting there and we're tempted just the same
But with the Bible we know there's a way, to return to God's heavenly fold
It's the best-selling book of all time, its wisdom grows not old

Read it and re-read it and try to understand
It's all about the relationship between our great God and man
There's so much more to this wonderful book, its truths have stood the test of time
It has the power to change your life, if read with open heart and mind

It's more than just a book. God speaks to us, you should read it every day
You'll come to see that Jesus is, the Truth, the Life, the Way
You'll transform from fan to follower as you read about the Lord
And you'll trust in His promises for the Bible is His Word

Prayer

*Thank you, Lord, for your Word. It is a guidebook for life, as
relevant today with powerful truths and life-giving wisdom. People
have not changed and we need this awesome book of transformation
as much today as ever, but we need eyes to see, ears to hear and a heart
and mind that is open to your Word. It's a love story with prophecies,
parables, poetry and reveals so much of You and how much You love
us. You are a wonderful God, who created us, who died for us and who
left your Word with us, so that we can find You and never be alone.*

Amen

Is it crazy to praise God for the consequences of using our free will?

We praise him for the gift of free will but do we ever stop and think about praising him for the suffering we go through, as a consequence of <u>not</u> using our free will wisely? Free will gives us the right to do anything or everything we want to, but that does not mean that everything is right for us.

Our God is NOT a helicopter parent, hovering over every little thing that we do, ready to step in to save us from the trouble we get ourselves into. Nor is He a lawnmower parent, ready to move every obstacle in our way, so that our path through life is smooth and easy.

He allows us to make mistakes and to deal with the consequences and that's something we learn early in our Christian walk. He has solutions and processes in place to help us get out of trouble, but we have to know His will, to believe and to follow His ways. He is always with us, ready to help if we pray and ask for His help. He is definitely NOT a helicopter parent.

"I have the right to do anything" you say –
but not everything is beneficial. "I have the right to do
anything" – but not everything is constructive."

1 Corinthians 10:23
(NIV)

God is not a helicopter parent

God is not a helicopter parent, nor is He a dictator
He's all about relationship, He *is* the great creator
He gave us life and free will too, put us above all living things
Made us in the image of God and delights in our well being

Like a good parent, God cares for us and wants us to grow to be
The best version of ourselves, living lives of peace
He does that by allowing mistakes, accidents and pain
And He's there to pick us up, when we fall again

He doesn't do, what we can do for ourselves, whatever that may bring
He doesn't cover us in bubblewrap, so we never feel a thing
He doesn't fight our battles for us, those things that block our path
He wants a two-way relationship and is there to help, when asked

He knows we need to overcome, troubles that come our way
Although it hurts him, He doesn't hover, but walks beside us every day
He's not a lawnmower parent that mows down every bad thing before it takes a hold
And he's not a dictator, who demands *His* way and we just do as we are told

He is the great God who loves us, who gave us life and freedom
To live our lives the way we want and hopefully lead us to His kingdom
He doesn't cast us all adrift to do the best we can
He gives us an instruction manual, the Bible, it's all part of His plan

He wants us to use the gifts He gave us, it's our responsibility
To use our minds and hearts to love and praise Him, for all eternity
He is a loving Father, Son and Holy Ghost
Not a helicopter or lawnmower parent, that's why we love Him most

I feel uncomfortable, almost crazy, for praising Jesus for the terrible circumstances of His death. He knew beforehand what was to happen and He still went to the Cross. I call it a beautiful ugliness.

It was the worst, the cruellest, the most unjust, humiliating act of savagery. He suffered at the hands of men who were driven by fear, jealousy and ruthless ambition. These men, the religious leaders, were prepared to do whatever it took to be rid of this newcomer, this nobody who claimed to be the son of God. His ministry was only three years, but in that time He built up a huge following who witnessed his miracles and heard His teaching. His followers believed He was the Messiah, who would overthrow Roman oppression. His enemies could see what was happening - He had to be stopped, so He was betrayed for pieces of silver and He suffered terribly and died on a Cross.

But His death led to a glorious triumph.

He rose on the third day and left no-one in any doubt that He was the Son of God, who came to earth to die for our sins as was prophesised 700 years before. He not only took our sins to the Cross, He left them there.

When He rose in glory, He rose with a New Covenant that says if we open our hearts to Him, confess our sins, ask for forgiveness and accept Him as our Lord and Saviour, He will give us the gift of eternal life. We will have a place in Heaven with Him and the angels and all our loved ones, who are found worthy at the final judgement.

The whole idea that He would do that for us is crazy.

He died so that we may live. I praise Him and I thank Him for His great love for us.

"For God so loved the world that He gave His one and only Son, that whoever believes in him shall not perish but have eternal life"

John 3:16
NIV

A Beautiful Ugliness

It's almost too incomprehensible for words, I can hardly take it in
That you would suffer and die on a Cross, to take away our sin
No guilt was found in you, yet they still took you away
To satisfy their ugly demands that you should die that day

Ugly men with ugly hearts who schemed to have you killed
Not comprehending that this one act, would see prophecy fulfilled
The ugliness of your betrayal and trial, the whipping and thorny crown
The beatings and burden and pain you endured, but you made not a sound

They hammered the nails in your hands and feet then raised your Cross on high
Naked now they divided your clothes and left you there to die
It was ugly. It was cruel. It was a travesty
I don't understand why you'd do it Lord, to go through this for me

Then on the third day it all made sense, your motive was so clear
You rose in glory from the grave and to your followers, appeared
Death was defeated, all doubts dispelled, everything you said you meant
You ushered in a new way to live and established a new covenant

Such a beautiful pledge you made to us, if, with loving hearts we come
You promise us eternal life to live in your heavenly kingdom
The paradox is beautiful Lord, you died to give us life - the idea is almost surreal
I don't understand why you'd do it Lord, for you get the worst of the deal

We get You and your guarantee if we believe, we'll be heaven bound
And you only get us, pitiful as we are, with all our ups and downs
Left to ourselves, we have no defence against Satan and all his evil ways
But Lord you'd thought of everything, when you rose in glory, on that day

You left your disciples filled with the Holy Spirit, to speak to all in their native tongue
To build your church and spread the good news that through you,
	our new life's begun
You showed the way with your Bible stories - of your good works,
	wisdom and life lessons
You've left the door always open for us, to seek you and make our confessions

Oh Lord! How beautiful is your love for us and how wonderful your resurrection
That gives us new life, new hope - if we follow your instruction
You went through all that you did, so that we could plainly see
The beautiful from the ugliness, of that day on Calvary

Prayer

Oh my awesome God. You are mighty. You are magnificent.

There is nothing You can't do.

You triumphed over evil. You chose the hardest way possible to show us the greatest love. You are God and You didn't have to do it that way, but you did, because we would not have believed any other way.

And you made sure we believed you, by rising from the grave to be seen not by a handful of people, but by over 500 people over a 30 day period. Awesome. You empowered your apostles with the gift of tongues, healing and miracles, to go throughout the World and preach the good news that Christ is risen and your church on earth began.

There is none like you Lord. You showed us what real love looks like, what hope feels like and how good life is, when we follow Your ways.

Lord, I believe you are everything You say you are:

The Bread of Life
The Light of the World
The Gate
The Good Shepherd
Tthe Way, the Truth and the Life
The True Vine

I love you Lord, I believe in You, I trust You completely.
Let nothing separate me from you ever.

Amen

DYSFUNCTION AND DISAPPOINTMENT

Is it crazy to praise God for a dysfunctional family? You might think so, but not really. It's the best environment for teaching you what you DON'T want in your life – incessant arguments, anger, fear, resentment, jealousy, tension, apathy, desperation.

It also teaches you - if you let God open your eyes and heart, about forgiveness, understanding, empathy, acceptance, self-control, peace, joy and love.

I wrote this poem thinking of the many people I've met in my life's journey that carry emotional scars from growing up in a dysfunctional family. People have different ways of dealing with dysfunction but whatever way they go, they are all impacted by it. From childhood to adulthood, those scars and memories will affect their decision making, their relationships, the way they see themselves and the way they see the world.

I've witnessed the healing and change in people when they find God and have Him in their lives, even in my own life. I'm convinced that God will, at some point, provide a way forward. For those who see it and embrace Him, their lives are forever changed, for the better.

If you believe in God, then pray. There is always hope that things will turn around and they often do. If you pray according to God's will, He will answer your prayers and when He doesn't it's because He has something better for you.

> *"The Lord is my Rock, my fortress and my deliverer;*
> *my God is my rock, in whom I take refuge,*
> *my shield and the horn of my salvation.*
> *He is my stronghold, my refuge and my Saviour"*

2 Samuel 22:2-3
(NIV)

Saved by Grace

"Hurting people hurt other people" that's what Joyce Meyer once said
And I pondered deeply on that, as the words swirled through my head
It brought to mind my childhood, a difficult one I recall
The fear and the tension and anger, it made no sense at all

I suffered many years witnessing, many of my parents' fights
The arguing was endless and would go on day and night
At times there was a point to it and other times unclear
Talking the same language, but neither willing to wait and hear

My mother would hold me tight and say 'forgive him, he's not that bad'
He's just got a few things going on, he's really a great dad"
My father would come to me and say "I really do love your mother
But she's awful hard to live with and we both love you and your brother"

Then there'd be the making up, the sobbing and the plea
'Don't know why we fight so much - please don't leave me'
It felt to me like their relationship, was really on the skids
And I'd hear them say we have to patch it up and be here for the kids

I often tried to figure them out, just what it was that drove them
But I was only just a kid - I didn't know then they were broken
My brother's way was to just switch off and focus on himself
The four of us were locked in pain and we all needed help

Then, I don't know how it happened, but Jesus came to stay
Like a new broom cleans a house, He swept our sins away
With God's help my parents learnt to be honest with each other
To speak their minds with kindness, as an example to me and my brother

It took a while but they finally reached, a peaceful state of life
Their energies poured into church, they'd lost the urge to fight
Their deep wounds healed, they loved us and knew they had to stop their war
and stay together for the kids, it was the right thing after all

I saw it all, the transformation to the light from darkest black
And I praise God for his handiwork that got them both on track
I thank God for the lessons learnt and for my family
Dysfunctional as we once were, now saved by grace and free.

What hurtful experiences did you suffer as a child?

Were there times when you prayed for someone to come and rescue you?

As you look back at your life, were there times that you can recognise now but you didn't recognise then, that God had intervened?

It gives you something to think about and helps to clarify your thinking by writing it down

Prayer

Father God, I praise you and thank you for everything you have done in my life.

From my childhood and the dramas and traumas; the things I saw and the things that were done to me. But it wasn't all bad and there were times of peace and happiness. As a young child I learnt about you but You were a distant God, who hadn't come to my rescue. As I grew into a teenager, I was too ashamed to keep you in my life, so I lived without You and lost my way.

I praise you and thank you for sticking with me. Even though for a long time I was far from you, You never gave up on me.

I praise you and thank you for being a perfect father, teacher, counsellor, protector and provider. You have walked beside me through my joys and sorrows. I realise now how hard I made my life by doing things in my rebellious way and it's only since I have found you again, that I see how life could have been.

Though I didn't know it, you were with me all the time and I am blessed by your love. You are a mighty God and I worship you and praise you.

Amen

The Lord is my shepherd, I lack nothing. He makes me lie down in green pastures. He leads me beside the quiet waters. He refreshes my soul and guides me along the right paths for his name's sake.

Event though I walk through the darkest valley, I will fear no evil for you are with me; your rod and your staff, they comfort me.

You prepare a table before me in the presence of my enemies. You anoint my head with oil, my cup overflows.

Surely goodness and love will follow me all the days of my life and I will dwell in the house of the Lord forever

Psalm 23
(NIV)

Is it crazy to praise God for the bad things that happen in our lives?

To give Him thanks for the difficulties and disasters, the mountains and the molehills we make into mountains, the chains we've had to break and challenges, we've had to face? Think about that, how we handled them at the time and what was the outcome.

I used to be one of those people who wouldn't say anything when I was upset, but then I'd go home and have sleepless nights having imaginary arguments that I never had the courage for, in the cold light of day. I'd be so stirred up, still angry and tired too. The battlefield in my mind would rage for days until the cold realization hit me, that I wasn't going to say or do anything. I was just going to bottle it all up inside, then seek relief through all kinds of things that in the end made the problems worse. I finally realized that wasn't the answer and I had to change my thinking..

Renewing our minds, to change our thinking from doing things our way to doing things His way is the answer. God should be our first resort, not the last.

I found that if we turn our problems _to_ God and ask Him to help, He will. He did for me, and I've changed and grown. With Him in my life I've found peace and forgiveness and honesty. I can speak up now from a position of love and confidence that He is with me and guiding me. Life is good but I couldn't have made the change in my own strength. That's what difficulties and disasters are for. It's God's way of testing our faith and watching if, what we have learnt about His ways, is being lived out in our lives. God is so good and I praise Him for showing me how to change my life, by changing my thinking, by the renewal of my mind. The "battlefield", the theatre of war in my mind, is now a place of peace.

"Do not conform to the pattern of this world but be
transformed by the renewing of your mind. Then you will be able
to test and approve what God's will is – his good, pleasing and perfect will'.

Romans 12:2
(NIV)

Change your Thoughts, Change your Life

There's a pathway in my thinking that I have often trod
Where my thoughts turn into feelings and I move away from God
I wander and I focus on the wrongs instead of right
And allow those negative thoughts and feelings, keep me awake all night

Those thoughts fuel my emotions and I really get upset
My anger turns into tears and I feel really stressed
I have all sorts of conversations, crazy plans and promises, to make things right
    next time
there's no place for rational thought in the battlefield of my mind

I ask myself why I feel so miserable? It's an effort to face each day
And I dig myself a great big hole and that's where I want to lay
Feeling sorry for myself, well, that's where Satan wants me to be
But not God, no - God wants me to be up and about and to live life joyfully

He wants me to enjoy my life, all the good and bad
the ups and downs, the twists and turns, He doesn't want me to be sad
Life's ups and downs is how we grow, it's important to have the right attitude
Trust in Him that it will all work out and have a sense of gratitude

Renew your mind is what I read, in the Bible the other day
For God will help us if we turn _to_ Him, He can't help - if we turn away
You can transform your negative thinking that was bringing you undone
With the power of Jesus on your side, your battles can be won.

Is it crazy to praise God for stubbornness?

That fierce independent streak that says 'I don't need any help I'll do it my way'. Even when we know we need help we won't ask. We just stress out, fall into depression and hope for a rescuer. When no-one comes, the depression goes deeper and we lose all hope. We think there is no way out. The sad thing is, the situation we find ourselves in, is self-imposed because of stubbornness. A vicious circle.

I'd come across an article written by an American author, Frederick Beuckner who talked about a person being so fiercely independent, that they couldn't accept help, even from God himself. The article is at the end of the poem. It really made me think where our personal independence comes from. Is it something that we learn from our parents, or something formed by our personal experiences? Is it about achievement or success, responsibility, ego or just plain belligerence? It made me look at my own life and there it was – a prideful stubbornness. Oh! how I've prayed to God to change me.

Refusal to seek help is either pride, fear, denial, or habit – you've fought so many of your own battles, for so long, you just don't know how to surrender. Or it's too hard and we are stuck in our stubbornness. Do you know that's pride? Oftentimes we refuse help because we're too proud to accept help, taking pride in always being able to do things for ourselves. Or, we're too embarrassed. We don't want people thinking that we can't do, whatever it is.

Pride doesn't make you happy. It makes you a captive. Pride can lead to all sorts of negative emotions – bitterness, self-pity, anger, regret. The Bible says "pride goeth before a fall" and you need that fall to be humbled.

"Pride goes before destruction, a haughty spirit before a fall"

Proverbs 16:18
(NIV)

Surrender

It's funny how life repeats itself, especially the mistakes
How sin and attitudes can be generational, that's how long it takes
Children see and do and learn, how their parents handled strife
It sets the foundation of who they become and their approach to life

As a child I watched my mother, facing life's storms and trials
I saw her rely on herself, through the really tough times
Even when her strength was spent she didn't pray, not that I recall
She thought she could do it by herself, she thought she could do it all

Independent, self-reliant that's what I came to understand
Mum didn't think to call on God – didn't need His helping hand
In my life, in the darkest times, I also, never thought to ask
Help from God to get me through, I was too focused on the task

With my mother's spirit of resilience, clenched fist determination and drive
I'd grit my teeth and see it through, that's how I've been through life
And my children were the same as me, I took some pride in that
I knew that I had made them strong, they'd never be a 'doormat'

But I was wrong as I came to see, I just didn't understand
the one thing a clenched fist can't do is accept, even from God himself, a helping
        hand[1]
I've come to see that stubborn pride is a long and lonesome road
The struggle never ending, steps weary from the load

It shouldn't be as hard as it is, to surrender all to Him
And ask for a helping hand, when times are tough and grim
It shouldn't be a great big deal, to get down, on our knees and pray
To humble ourselves before Him, ask for help or show the way

Stubborn pride can lead to poor choices, that gets us further into strife
It defeats God's plan and purpose as we choose a lesser life
It puts up walls around us till our problems can't be sorted

[1]   (2019) Beuckner, Frederick. Media Blog "Humanly Blessed" January 15, 2019. First published
       (1982) in "The Sacred Journey" Harper San Francisco

Trapped in our life-experience, our thinking gets distorted

It cuts us off and we'll never know if there were other options
We'll never know because we never thought to ask, God with all His wisdom
Even though you can't see God, He's always there, to help us find the answers
So open your heart and let Him come in, humble yourself and surrender.

Frederick Beuchner, an American author said.

"To do for yourself the best that you have it in you to do - to grit your teeth and clench your fists in order to survive the world at its harshest and worst – is, by that very act, to be unable to let something be done for you and in you that is more wonderful still.

The trouble with steeling yourself against the harshness of reality is that the same steel that secures your life against being destroyed secures your life also, against be opened up and transformed by the holy power that life comes from.

You can survive on your own. You can grow strong on your own. You can even prevail on your own. But you cannot become human on your own. Surely that is why, in Jesus' sad joke, the rich man has as hard a time getting into Paradise as that camel through the needle's eye because with his credit card in his pocket, the rich man is so effective at getting for himself everything he needs that he does not see that what he needs more than anything else in the world, can be had only as a gift. He does not see that the one thing a clenched fist cannot do is accept, even from God himself, a helping hand"

Prayer

Father God, I praise you for the wisdom you instil in others, the gift of insight that they share with the world.

Lord, bless Frederick Beuckner who has discovered a deep truth about our human nature. Stubborness and pride are in each and every one of us, especially in me.

I even denied I was like that, I dressed it up as being "fiercely independent". I was proud of being able to do things for myself and stubbornly refused help, even when I so desperately needed help. Those things are childish and like a child, I used them as a defence against the world. It was the only bit of power I felt I had.

Lord, I pray that you will help me overcome my fear, so that I can be brave; overcome my pride that I can be humble; overcome my denial of reality that I can come to see that I cannot do things in my own strength, but with your help I can do what I need to do.

My wonderful Lord, I pray that you will help me change my ways, that I see clearly the bad habits I have and create new ones in me, habits that honour You and ones that will lead me to the better life that You promise.

Amen

Is it crazy to praise God for a hard life?

A life that began badly and went downhill from there. You've had to fight, fight, fight for every little bit of progress as you dragged yourself up, trying to be a better person and not let things drag you back down. You've always felt alone. No-one to help. No-one who understood your pain or what you've been through. Whether those struggles were perceived or real, they were real to you and you're exhausted.

Yes, it is crazy to praise God in those circumstances but did you know that if you are still striving to be a better person, to live the better life, God has been with you all the time? You've just not seen Him. You've not seen the many times He has sent the right person at the right time, with the right words to encourage you, to help you, to protect you, to guide you.

I was inspired to write this poem for every person who has had to struggle and fight to be the person God wants you to be. To live out the plan He has for your life.

Turn to Him and you will find the peace, love, security and purpose you so desperately need. Your struggles may not cease, but with God purposefully in your life, you will find peace in your circumstances and strength to overcome what needs to be overcome.

He cares for you. He created you and you are meant to be here. Perhaps He's used your struggles to inspire others; to be a good example to your children, to your friends, to your work colleagues; perhaps He was trying to teach you something that you have not quite learnt yet. He answers prayers and there is a better life waiting, if you follow Him.

"For I know the plans I have for you," declares the Lord, "plans to prosper you and not to harm you, plans to give you hope and a future"

Jeremiah: 29:11
(NIV)

There Once was a Girl

There once was a girl who fought and fought -

- In the womb for her right to life
- As a child for her right to be cared for
- As a young girl for her right to be protected
- As a teenager for her right to matter
- As a young woman for her right to be heard
- As a mature woman for her right to be respected
- As an old woman for her right to be seen

She didn't have to fight but that was all she knew so she –

- Relied on herself, wouldn't ask for help. Even if she could, she wouldn't
- Thought her independence would protect her from betrayal, failures, lies and let-downs
- Made mistakes, misjudged others and had many other hurts
- Self-contained, self-managed, self-medicated, self-harmed

The years of fighting, the years of toughening, left scars

- Trusting no-one; Defensive
- A coiled spring waiting, anticipating the criticism, condemnation
- Made to feel not good enough, never enough

She resisted God yet through God's grace she's still here

- He made a way for her when there was no way
- He lifted her up with His grace and carried her time and time and time again

What she sought she found in the world, but it was temporary. Only God can give her what she wanted – a lasting, ever faithful love, complete security, and purpose

He waited. Patiently. and I prayed for that girl. Diligently

I prayed for that girl, that Jesus the Good Shepherd, would find His lost lamb and bring her to his flock where she would learn how it feels to be truly loved, to know the freedom of complete and utter trust in a loving, personal, opening up relationship with God. To be valued for her, not for her material things, not for the good things she's done, or what she's achieved – they are of this world.

I said to God 'she's not lost because she's angry or rebellious – she's lost because she doesn't know how to surrender; doesn't know how to put her fists down and her hands up and would never think to cry out, "Help Me Jesus, I can't do this by myself anymore"

I prayed for that girl that she would know the peace of God, which passes all understanding. I prayed that she would learn, with Jesus in her heart, that you don't have to fight alone. God is with you and for you. There *is* victory in Jesus.

And God answered my prayers. There once was a girl

FRUITS OF THE SPIRIT - JOY

Call me crazy but I praise God for everything and especially for the joy He has brought to my life. The ecstatic almost euphoric delight in all things, despite what's going on around me. Things like waking up in the morning. Even though my body is older, slower and sometimes painful, it's still a joy to wake up, to still be here.

To look at my loved ones, from babies to grown-ups. My eyes fill with joyful tears to see a connection, a loving thread of relationship that joins us as family and friends. I watch the news of this troubled world and I am still joyous because my hope is in the Lord. My future rests with Him.

Joy is not to be confused with happiness. Happiness is an emotion and temporary.

In the biblical context Joy is an attitude, a way of living. It's not a "thing" you can buy or watch on tv. It's not something that can be forced on you, or something you can fake. It's not dependent on your circumstances or other people, or the amount of money you have in the bank.

Joy is an attitude of the heart. You choose Joy. It is an integral part of who you are and it's an important, invaluable tool, to help us face the challenges of life. God has promised that for those who believe in Him, joy will be their reward.

"Be full of joy always. I will say again, be full of joy.
Let your gentleness be evident to all. The Lord is near.
Do not be anxious about anything, but in every situation
by prayer and petition, with thanksgiving, present your requests to God.
And the peace of God, which transcends all understanding
will guard your hearts and your minds in Christ Jesus"

Philippians 4:4-7
(NIV)

Finding and Keeping Joy

Thank you Lord for your promise, that if I believe I'll have your joy
That almost inexpressible delight nothing on earth can destroy
Thank you, Lord, for your Bible - every word is true
About how to find joy and keep it, in everything I do
About how to make it part of me, part of who I am
Thank you, Lord, for the joy in my life, a blessing in your great plan

You have a plan for each of us and as we live and learn
that you are there to guide and help us, whichever way we turn
Some of us find you early and have you in our hearts
Others spend tormented years seeking that narrow path
And when they do, their joy is great, they live with chains unbound
Released from all their suffering, because it's you they found

Joy is a way of believing, of always looking for the good
Turning things from bad to better, as God said it would
Once I shook off all the heartaches, the sorrow and the pain
The will to live, not just to survive, has bloomed in me again
Joy can take my darkest days and turn them into light
Because I believe that with God's help, I will be all right

For me joy has locked and blocked out fear and doubt and insecurity
I feel it in the fullness of trust, in God's love for me
God wants us to enjoy our lives, the journey that we're on
To taste and see and celebrate, the earth we walk upon
Joy is such a blessing, a weapon against despair
It's a feeling like no other, so choose it if you dare.

Is it crazy to praise God for turbulence?

Have you ever been in a plane that's struck turbulence? How that plane pitches and rolls, shakes and shudders, you think the wings are going to fall off and you'll be heading for the ground at any minute. You look around and passengers are wild-eyed and white-knuckled, yet the flight attendants are going about their tasks and in quiet tones, offer comfort. The pilot too, gets on with the job and all of a sudden, the plane lifts and levels out and it's all smooth again.

I was travelling to Sydney to visit family and I felt the aircraft shudder as we hit some turbulence. I watched the flight attendants reassure the passengers, then the captain's voice came over the intercom. He was calm, confident, I felt safe and as we left the turbulence and flew in calm skies, I thought about what we had just been through. Before we landed the poem had been written and it's one of my favorites.

Think of the plane as how our lives are – shaken and bruised, battered by life's storms. But God is not. He's calm, relaxed and in control.

Think of the pilot and flight attendants, knowing what to do to respond, to give us hope and something to hang onto. If we didn't hit turbulence we wouldn't be aware of who is there to help us and of who is in control. We are comforted and reassured by their actions.

That's the same as the comfort and peace we feel knowing God is in control through all our turbulence. Let's hand over our fears, anxieties and worries and let God take care of it.

> *"Praise be to the God and Father of our Lord Jesus Christ,*
> *the Father of compassion, the God of all comfort, who comforts*
> *us in all our troubles, so that we can comfort those in any*
> *trouble with the comfort we ourselves receive from God"*

2 Corinthians 1:3-5
(NIV)

> *"Cast your cares upon the Lord; for He careth for you"*

1 Peter 5:7
(NIV)

Safety Instructions

Airlines seem to have it right "Put on your seat belt and pull it tight
If we strike trouble pull down your mask - help yourself first and do it fast
Bend yourself forward and brace for the bumps, trust in the pilot to get through
    the humps
Follow instructions every step of the way - we're here to help you stay safe today"

Pretty simple really, when you think it through
when you're in a heap of trouble and don't know what to do
There's the calm and friendly voice, coming over the intercom
"please follow the safety instructions and we will get you home"

God's like that. He's left instructions on how to get through life
And he's gifted many people to instruct you, on how to do things right
There's your parents and your teachers and your mentors and your friends
Pastors and preachers, good people in your life, the list just never ends

They say "seek redemption for your sins and follow the way of the Lord"
This will save you from destruction when you decide to live in His Word
Then you can help others, as you come alongside them in their pain
To give them comfort and direction to live in the world again

Remember in all this to save yourself first
Then you can help others, when you're strong in God's Word
Your help is more effective as you come alongside
Cause you've listened, learnt and endured, come through it and survived

When you're born you get a ticket on this aeroplane called life
And it will take you on a journey full of lows and highs
Learn the "safety instructions" and on them become dependent
And you'll be great at helping others – being God's flight attendant

Is it crazy to praise God for you?

For the unique person that you are? Did you know there is no-one else on the earth who is exactly the same as you? You keep comparing yourself to others, but take a minute to think about this - out of the billions of people on this planet there is only one you. That's an awesome thought. You don't have to be better than anyone else, you just have to be the best *you* can be.

Have you ever thought about how wonderfully made you are? How God designed you, gave you life and blessed you with your own special way of thinking, of doing, of being. You could have ten brothers and sisters, all brought up in the same household, but you are not identical. None of them think the way you do, none of them do what you do. You are not a carbon copy of them nor are they of you.

If he didn't make you perfect, you are still perfect in His eyes.

Once you accept that, you can love yourself as you are. Once you do that, you will be able to love others, just as they are. Through this process you grow and receive the fruits of the spirit – love, peace, joy, to name a few.

God made you the way you are for a reason. Once you work out what that reason is, you will have found your purpose and I pray you will pursue that wholly and joyfully.

Did you know you are meant to be here? He wants the world to see you as He made you and He wants you to use the special gifts He gave you, for His glory.

"I praise you because I am fearfully and wonderfully made.
Your works are wonderful, I know that full well.

My frame was not hidden from you when I was made in the secret
place, when I was woven together in the depths of the earth.

Your eyes saw my unformed body; all the days ordained for me
were written in your book before one of them came to be.

Psalm 139: 14-16
(NIV)

Uniquely and Wonderfully Made

Uniquely and wonderfully made, and what the Bible says is true
God is the great Creator and He made only one of you
He put you here for a season, or for a reason and that's for you to find
Some will find their purpose early, for others it takes a lifetime

So be aware that God is there, to help you on your way
To live your life the best you can and praise Him every day
Thank Him for your character, the way you look, the way you think and speak
The life you've led, the love you have, the people that you meet

They watch the way you respond when troubles come, as they do to everyone
With strength and courage you lift yourself, to make sure the job gets done
They see the way you carry your sorrow, when you're hurt deep inside your heart
And they marvel at your steadfast faith that keeps you from falling apart

People see you with friends and family, making sure that they're ok
And they wonder at your inner peace and how you stay that way
You've just come to accept yourself and you've only got God to please
You can get on and live a happy life, all your fears released

Do you rise to face each new day, leaning into the wakening dawn
wondering what the day will bring, it's there new hope is born
Your attitude determines these things, your mind can sink you or save
Have you done your best and stayed upbeat, as through your life you've aged

So celebrate the things you like about yourself and forget the things you do not
For God made you unique and wonderful with the giftings that you've got
There is no-one else like you, remind yourself every day
God loves you as you are, uniquely and wonderfully made

Is there such a thing as random chance? Not if you believe in God. With God it is neither random, nor chance, but a deliberate choice He has made for you.

I know that sounds crazy, but if you believe in God, then you believe that He has a great plan for your life. As part of that plan He places you in situations, good and bad and He sends people into your life to lead, love, challenge, and be good examples for you to follow.

One such person in my life is Annette from Church on the Rise (COTR) at Maleny. Annette is the leader of the Women of Worth (WOW) group that meets every fortnight to do Bible study and to socialise. Annette preaches at church sometimes and is a wonderful, caring friend. God's light shines from her. I couldn't help but honour her by writing this poem.

Annette is the epitome of a person who manifests the fruits of the spirit—a joyful example of a godly woman. Everyone needs an Annette in their life.

When you meet a person who bears the fruits of the spirit, praise God for them and thank Him for sending them into your life.

"But the fruit of the Spirit is love, joy, peace, forebearance,
kindness, goodness, faithfulness
gentleness and self-control. Against such things there is no law".

Galatians 4:22-23
(NIV)

Quiet Angel

I know a quiet angel who is peaceful, loyal and true
a wonderful woman of God, who shares with us His good news
She's always there with a welcoming smile, as we meet together at WOW
A quiet achiever and true believer, an important part of our COTR crowd

Her quietness is not meekness, there is resilience and strength
her life has not been perfect, but with God it's been perfectly spent
She's like a soothing balm to the troubled soul, she knows just what to say
with words of encouragement or words of comfort, to help us through our day

She speaks God's Word at church or at WOW, in a way that is simple and clear
her words go deep within the hearts of all who are willing to hear
With the word of God to guide her, she is the epitome of grace
her life is God, church and family, the love is shining from her face

I know a quiet angel, working in our church community
ready to help or speak God's Word, wherever she is needed
How God lives in us, you can see in our dear Annette
A beautiful woman of God, our Leader and our friend.

GRIEF AND LOSS

Is it crazy to praise God for the death of loved one? To thank Him for the blessing of the child He has just taken away. It's hard to get your mind around that one.

We often curse God and in our anger we ask Him why/ why? Why your child / husband / loved one? Why not someone less deserving, who has lived the full score of their years while your child / husband/ loved one still had their best years ahead.

We don't understand and find it hard to accept. It is in God's timing and out of our hands. So we praise Him for the change that happens in our lives as we adjust to the new reality. That can be a painful journey, but if we trust God and turn to Him, when we have passed through grief, we are what He has led us to become.

My youngest daughter Kate passed away on 9th July, 2016. She was 48 and had been diagnosed Stage 4 bowel cancer three years previously.

I thank God every day for those extra precious three years He gave her. In those three years we drew closer as family. We were able to share some great times with Kate, "making memories" she would say. Although she was dying, she showed us how to live gracefully, gratefully and fully in the moment.

Since Kate passed, feathers would appear, seemingly out of nowhere. It became a family thing as we all felt the appearance of a feather meant she dropped by to say hello. I thank God and praise Him for his mercy and kindness to me with the feathers. They are a constant reminder that He and Kate are always near.

"The Lord is close to the brokenhearted and saves
those who are crushed in spirit"

Psalms 34:18
(NIV)

The Feather on the Floor

When my youngest daughter passed away, I lived in a world of pain
It was a world of endless sadness knowing I'd never see her again
I was so sorry for the times I'd let her down, or let my work come before her
though it was stretched sometimes it was never broken, that bond between mother
    and daughter

Oh how we all grieved. I was so far down, right at the end of my tether
I prayed for a sign, a message from her, then I started seeing these feathers
They'd appear out of nowhere, on our clothes, on our bags, on the ground
Desperate we were, we believed it was her, letting us know she was still around

It became a family thing, "Kate's here!" we'd say when we saw one
Always at times we were thinking of her and the many things that she'd done
Or they'd appear when our hearts were so saddened, remembering our final goodbyes
And they'd make our hearts be gladdened, we'd say 'Kate's dropped in to say hi"

We celebrated the special occasions, like her birthday, her passing and at Christmas
It comforts and helps us heal, to feel she is still with us
This year, it meant so much to me, more than words could ever say
When I found a feather on the floor, in the house, on Mother's Day

No-one put it there I knew and all the windows and doors were shut
But there it was and as I knelt on the floor, I prayed before picking it up
"Thank You God and thank you Kate, for this wonderful surprise!"
My heart was bursting with love for them both, tears just flowed from my eyes

Four years ago she left us, the cancer took her on the 9th of July
There's not a day that goes by I don't think of her, how she loved, how she cared,
    how she died
I thank God for her life and the extra three years, God gave her, how I wish it could
    have been more
Still, I'm so happy and I'm so grateful for finding Kate's feather on the floor.

Have you ever had that crazy feeling where you are compelled to say something? The words just bubble up and are in your mouth. You don't really understand what's happening and the words are ones that you aren't sure you want to say.

You think the person you're talking to will object, or get angry, or get upset. So you hesitate, fighting the urge because you really don't know what's going to come out and then you say it.

That's God leading you.

That's God putting the words in your mouth that will change someone's life. You don't think that at the time, but it will and it does.

I praise God for that revelation. I praise God and thank Him for putting the words in my mouth that have given people peace, comfort, and a place in heaven as they confessed their sins, asked for forgiveness and accepted Jesus as their Lord and Saviour. It is life-changing for them and confirms and grows my faith that the words of my mouth can heal and save. Thank you Jesus.

> *"If you declare with your mouth, "Jesus is Lord" and believe in your heart that God raised him from the dead, you will be saved.*
>
> *For it is with your heart that you believe and are justified, and it is with your mouth that you profess your faith and are saved"*

Romans 10: 9-10
(NIV)

> *Very truly I tell you, the one who believes has eternal life"*

John 6:47
(NIV)

The Words of my mouth

Let the words of my mouth praise you oh Lord, let them say
    what you want me to say
Let them calm a grieving mother and soothe her pain away
Let them be words of comfort, when her world has fallen apart
Let them be words of kindness, to lift her spirit and heal her heart

Lord, let me know the time to speak, when a friendly word is needed
Let me know just what to say, let no cries for help go unheeded
Fill me with awareness, to choose the one who needs you most
And let me tell them about you - the Father, Son and Holy Ghost

Let me tell them about You, how your love for us does not cease
Let me tell them of your story and of your eternal peace
How Jesus walked upon the earth and left our sins there, on the cross
Then rose again in glory, with a new covenant, to save the lonely and the lost

This new covenant that says, God asks us to believe in Him
To seek him with all our heart, have faith and confess our sins
Humble ourselves and ask forgiveness, pray as you've never prayed before
And we'll receive eternal life, to spend with our Lord and Saviour

For those who mourn

Let the words of my mouth tell of this promise, every word is true
For believers or non believers, Jesus died to give it to you
Let me tell them of the comfort that it brings to those of us, left behind
To know our loved one has been saved and is in heaven for all time

Oh! the peace it brings, to know our loved one, is in a far far better place
Spending eternity with Jesus, to feel His love and know His grace
Let the words of my mouth uphold this truth, that gives hope to every Christian
That you'll meet your loved one again in heaven, when your time on earth is done

For those who struggle

To those who feel they can't go on, their burden is too heavy, the struggle is too long
They feel so alone, there's no-one who cares, let the words of my mouth stop them
    right there

Lord, guide my words, let me be kind, to rebuild their trust and renew their minds
To believe that you are with them each day, to lean on with faith and
 turn to and pray

Let the words of my mouth remind them that you, carried your cross and all you
 went through
Let me say that each life has its own difficult seasons and if prayers are unanswered
 you have your reasons
Let me strengthen their faith, help them stand tall, they *can* do all things through
 You Lord, who empowers us all
Help me to show that to endure is to please, with unbreakable faith, their burdens
 will cease

For those who pray for their loved ones to be saved
So often hearts are heavy, when loved ones go astray
and the only thing that they can do is get on their knees and pray
Lord, help me to lead them in prayer with words that will touch Your Heart
As we call on your mercy for their loved ones, to give them a brand new start

Lord, help me to comfort and reassure, that you are always near
That they can talk to you about anything, all their worries and their fears
Let the words of my mouth speak of your great love that pours out for the lost and
 the broken
To give them hope their loved one can be saved, through the words that are spoken

Prayer

Heavenly Father, Jesus, Holy Spirit, God three-in-one, Almighty God, I praise
you and thank you for the words you put in my mouth when the need arises.

I praise you and thank you that you send to me, people who
need words of comfort, words of encouragement, words that
clarify and calm. Words that will lead them to you.

Lord, I thank you and praise for the wonderful gift you have
given me to be able to speak Your Name into their hearts and
minds; to plant the seeds of belief, faith and hope.

Words are powerful and I pray I will always be mindful of how
words can impact lives. I pray that you always guide me to know just
what to say and when. Sometimes silence is all I need to do. Just to listen
and let your love flow through and over the person who needs you.

Lord, I thank you and praise you as the great God who loves us all.

Amen

Is it crazy to praise God for heaven?

Some people think so. Some people think Christians are crazy to believe there is a God in Heaven and He knows us all by name and watches over us.

Their view is, people are born, they live, they die. Whether that life is short or long, successful or not, whether it's lived, or was just an existence on this planet, when we get to the end, that's it. End of story.

But I praise God that He promises there is a heaven and that those who believe in Him, will share in the eternal life, with Him. I praise Him that He promises heaven is a place of peace, where there is no more pain, no more suffering, no more tears, no more worry, or striving. We rest in perfect peace and love.

That thought has comforted me when loved ones have passed and it inspired me to write this poem. I was thinking of good people that I knew that had recently passed and how they were godly people in this life. The thought of heaven keeps me striving to live God's way in this life, so I can join Him and my loved ones in the next. God is a promise keeper.

"He will wipe away every tear from their eyes. There will be no more death, or mourning or crying or pain, for the old order of things has passed away"

Revelation 21:4
(NIV)

I Like to Think There is a Heaven

I like to think there is a heaven, a place of peace where our loved ones go
As they pass from this life to the next and say goodbye to those below
A place where God is there to greet them, He knows their name and
    what they've done
Their brief earthly life is over, the eternal life begun

I like to think there is a heaven, a place of rest at end of life
No more aches and pains of ageing, gone are worries, fear and strife
Released from burdens - shackles snapped and blown away
Free at last to walk with lightness, looking forward to each new day

He shows them round His heavenly mansion and to their room He has prepared
Filled with love and music and laughter and all their loved ones waiting there
Oh what joy to be reunited, with loved ones departed long before
Oh what joy to be with the Father, the God they've worshipped and adored

With that joy there is a sadness as they see our tears shed on earth below
They whisper "I'm ok" but we can't hear them, they're gone – that's all we know
As we search our hearts for answers, why them? Why now? Why this way?
We're comforted by the hope of heaven and that we'll meet again, someday

God said the path to heaven is not easy - not by works, but living by faith
If that's you, He's saved a spot for you, in that wonderful place
I like to think there is a heaven, that life on earth is not all there is
God promises more to all believers, to those who declare we are His

Is it crazy to praise God for cemeteries and memorials, for flower laden telegraph poles and small crosses on the side of the road?

It seems such a macabre thought but I don't see these places as morbid reminders. Instead, I praise God for those special places that help us remember and honour our loved ones who have passed.

One such place is St Margaret's Anglican Church at Woombye. They have a Memorial Garden where you can sit and reflect on loved ones passed. There are small plaques pinned to the structure, bearing the names of deceased parishioners. It's a beautiful place and I wanted to share this with you through the words of this poem.

It's a source of great comfort to visit those special places. To sit awhile and bring fresh flowers, to weep and talk to our loved ones passed as if they could hear. God hears us and sees our sorrow. He comforts those who mourn.

I praise God for that spirit within us, as human beings, to treat these places as holy ground, with respect, with reverence. They hold our loved ones, our memories, our what ifs, our dreams of what could have been and what was.

Our loved ones are at rest.

"Blessed are the poor in spirit, for theirs is the kingdom of heaven.
Blessed are those who mourn, for they will be comforted.

Matthew 5: The Beatitudes 3-4
(NIV)

Resting in the Arms of God

There's a special place in Woombye that human hands have made
A place where you can stop a while and sit there in the shade
It's St Margaret's Memorial Garden, a special place to reflect
On the life of your loved ones departed and what their love for you, meant

Here you can sit and remember and let the tears fall from your eyes
As you feel the loss so deeply and try to get on with your life
It's here you can feel the presence of God, come to heal your broken heart
And your heart is heavy as you gaze at the name, written on a little blue plaque

Such a small thing that means so much, to remember them this way
A permanent marker that means much more, than words could ever say
Affixed to a simple structure, to make their names easy enough to find
Put up for the loved ones gone, by the ones who are left behind

St Margaret's Memorial Garden, a place of remembrance, where the world just
      melts away
Sheltered In the shadow of St Margaret's Church, where your loved ones came to pray
They sought the Lord's mercy and forgiveness and their burdens became lighter to
      bear
Be glad for them now, in a much better place, peaceful in God's care

As you sit in the arbour look at the flowers, symbols of beauty and love
That's how to think of the precious life lost, now in heaven above
They'd be happy that you remember and wouldn't want you to feel all alone
As long as they are in your heart, they are never truly gone

So come and sit and rest awhile, let the memories fill your heart
Know that God's beside you as you walk that lonely path
It doesn't matter if you cry or laugh, passers-by won't think it odd
They'll see the sign and sympathise, believing too your loved one is now resting in
      the arms of God

It's crazy these days to think that Dads don't matter, because they do.

In this modern world, it's easy to get caught up in thinking that men and women are the same, they're interchangeable and that people no longer care about who does what. That wasn't God's plan.

God specifically designed men and women to be different from each other, fit for the purposes He had in mind. Men are to be the fathers of children, women to be the mothers. The differences are not just physical. Men and women think differently and have different emotional and spiritual responses. Their differences don't make them inferior. Their roles are equally important and should complement not compete with each other. That's a wonderful thing for a child. To have two parents, who can bring a complete and complementary range of physical, mental, emotional and spiritual examples, influences and responses to that child's life. I'm not thinking about what adults want, I'm thinking about what a child needs.

I was thinking of young families, of first-time fathers when I wrote this poem. It's such a big responsibility and family life as we know it has changed dramatically. There is a lot of shared parenting and fathers are encouraged to be involved with their children, instead of the distant provider of times past. Children learn from their parents, so fathers need to set a good example. There will be sacrifices to make, but with God's grace and goodness a father's legacy will be his influence for good in the lives of his children and generations to come. The greatest gift a good father can give is to bring his children up knowing who God is, how much He loves us and how true are His promises. The blessed child is the one with a loving father here on earth and in heaven.

"As for me and my household, we will serve the Lord"

Joshua 24:15
(NIV)

Dads Do Matter

Let me take a moment to tell you of your worth
Now that this little child, your flesh and blood, has come into the world
Your child is a gift, you are the father, you've got a big responsibility
To be the kind of father, your child wants and needs you to be

The moment you first hold your child and promise them your love
Is the moment you should take a minute, to thank our God above
He's given you this child to care for, to nurture and to mould
Cherish their journey, be involved and your own joy will unfold

So, fathers teach your children, show them how our good God works
Instil faith and hope and understanding, for a good life here on earth
Be an example of God's love, of forgiveness and of mercy
Be someone they can trust and turn to, when their own lives get a little murky

Teach them how to do things, sensibly, with calmness and with diligence
They'll learn the triumph of achievement and learn how to be patient
Show them respect and authority, your job is to help them stand on
        their own two feet
Your role is different from their mother's, it should complement not compete

Have a close relationship with your kids, be involved as best you can
It takes more than strength and courage, to be a good Dad and a man
Show them how much you love and respect their mother, children learn from
        watching you
What they see will reflect in their relationships, so be mindful, of what you say and do

Dads do matter, it matters so much, to teach them about God's ways
They'll carry that knowledge in their hearts to their end of days
That's the greatest gift you can bestow and that's how they'll remember you
Just like God our Father, ever loving and forgiving, ever faithful, ever true.

Is it crazy to praise God for churches?

With services online and Bible apps on mobile phones; with messaging through social media and streaming services, it is so easy these days to not see the necessity of going to church. Yet, there is something wonderful about being in God's House. Something special about sharing that time with other believers, spending time in God's presence and worshipping Him.

Some churches are so spirit-filled, you feel it the moment you step inside but if you never go, you'll never know.

Many churches are hundreds of years old and have a special place in the life of a community. Generations of families have attended the same church and their lives are interwoven into the life of the church.

One such church is St Margaret's Anglican Church in Woombye, a village on the Sunshine Coast. It's a wonderful little church with a great history and still has its own bell.

There's something special about the ringing of a church bell and the St Margaret's bell had been silenced for many years after vandals damaged it. Thanks to the efforts of the Friends of St Margaret's Committee, congregation and volunteers, the bell was repaired in 2018. It now rings out every second Sunday, five minutes before the service starts at 9.30am.

"Make a joyful noise to the Lord all the earth! Serve the Lord with gladness!
Come into His presence with singing? Know that the Lord, He is God.
It is He who made us and we are His; we are His people and the sheep
of His pasture. Enter His gates with thanksgiving and His courts with
praise! Give thanks to Him; and bless His Name! for the Lord is good; His
steadfast love endures forever, and His faithfulness to all generations"

Psalm 100
(NIV)

St Margaret's Church Bell

I heard the church bell ringing at St Margaret's church today
And I felt the Lord was calling all his people to come and pray
That sweet solemn sound of the ringing has not been heard for years
And as it carried through the morning air, I was reduced to tears

It brought me back to long ago, when as a child I went
To Sunday School with lots of kids and to church, with both my parents
Mum and Dad they loved the Lord and brought us up the same
Now many years on I still go to church, but everything else has changed

Happy days they were back then, we knew just where we stood
We learnt about love and forgiveness and the difference between bad and good
We ate proper meals at the proper time and in bed by 8 o'clock
Mum made us breakfast every morning, while we cleaned our shoes and put on
    socks

The world's so much different now, no-one's got time for anything
I've still got my friends at St Margaret's and that lovely bell that's ringing
There's something in that special sound that commands us all to come
To God's House, under God's roof, where we who are many are one

Oh! Thank You Lord for this gift of sound that calls us to Your side
Where peace and love is all around and where in You, we abide
Thank you God, for this gift of place where we worship here by choice
St Margaret's church in Woombye has finally found its voice.

Is it crazy to praise God for Companion Animals?

To praise Him for the blessing and the healing that companion animals bring to the bruised, the broken, the broken-hearted, the lost, the lonely, the sick, the injured, the grieving; the people with disabilities, the people with mental health issues and to millions of people all over the world, who just through life, find it too hard to completely love and trust another human being, but love and trust their pets. How could you not praise God for that?

That's not being crazy – that's being grateful, that God loves us so much, He found the perfect gift. He found a way to show His love for us, in a way we could accept, by giving us companion animals.

We love our animals because we see God manifested in them. We don't realise that's why we love them. It sounds crazy but it's not. We see unconditional love, forgiveness, faithfulness, the desire for relationship with us, the desire to be with us and accept us just as we are, imperfect, flawed and faulty. We see no condemnation, no judgement and we see truth. Animals do not lie.

And the way they love us – absolutely, unconditionally, totally – just as God loves us. And they teach us so many things - how to love and how to accept love; to look beyond ourselves and care for another living being; to know joy and sorrow; to teach us things about ourselves that we would never have learnt any other way; to be our good companion and to teach us to let go, when their time comes. The growing popularity of equine therapy and mind dogs for people with disabilities / mental health is acknowledging that animals have more than a functional value, they are our companions, carers and therapists. I thank God every day for them.

Our God is magnificently merciful and loving and kind. He knew what He was doing when He created the world and all that is in it. He placed humankind below Himself but above everything else, to have authority and stewardship over the earth, all the animals, the birds, sea creatures, and the plants. We are to care for His creation.

"Then God said, "Let us make mankind in our image, in our likeness, so that they may rule over the fish in the sea and the birds in the sky, over the livestock and all the wild animals, and over all the creatures that move along the ground"

Genesis 1:26
(NIV)

Our Good Companions

Oh my Lord! you are so clever, this gift that you've designed
To heal our broken hearts and clear our troubled minds
You are the great God of mercy, you know exactly what needs to be done
To fill that empty space within our lives, you give us a friend and companion

So we thank you for companion animals, for the joy and healing they bring
For the relationship, laughter and smiles, they really are a blessing
We learn to love them as they grow and watch them play and sleep and eat
Their love for us stirs an inner glow, they make our lives complete

To us they're more than pets, they're our therapists and friends
We can't help but love and care for them and we'll love them to the end
We tell them our troubles and they listen, but do not give any advice
Just love us with unconditional love to make us feel all right

Our constant confidantes and companions as we journey through life's way
They're always so happy to see us, it brightens up our day
The lessons they were sent to teach us, we wouldn't accept from You
So You wrapped them in our good companions so the lessons could get through

Oh God! I praise you for your thoughtfulness, for finding a brilliant solution
To the problems of a Godless world, with its shaky love and confusion
One thing is clear and You show us your love, You show us every day
With the wag of a tail, a trill, purr or whinny, of the pets you sent our way

When we lose a pet, or have to leave them behind, we grieve
over the lost relationship, that special bond we shared.

The story of Bill Hayward

My husband, Peter, is a horse handler, trainer, farrier, instructor, educator
and is well known on the Sunshine Coast, having been involved in working
with horses and donkeys for over thirty years. He does a lot of hoof trimming
and one of Peter's clients, Bill Hayward, had Peter trim Bill's donkeys' feet on
a regular basis. Bill had three donkeys, Maggie, Trilby and Boo. He let us take
Maggie and Trilby to be the donkeys in Nativity Plays at various churches over
the Christmas period, so we knew the donkeys and Bill Hayward, well.

Out of the blue we had a call from Bill's son, who told us his father had been
taken ill suddenly and was in hospital. He said that Bill didn't have much time
left and told us that Bill's last wish was to see his beloved donkeys once more.
He asked us if we would be able to transport the donkeys up to the hospital, to
make Bill's last wish come true. We were happy to do it.

God was there and blessed Bill with a perfect day. He blessed Bill with a gather-
ing of family and friends and He blessed us all, to witness the love and relationship between Bill and his donkeys. They knew him. They were happy to stand
and be stroked and petted by him for as long as he was able. Their presence
gave Bill so much joy and I praise God for the opportunity to grant Bill's Last
Wish.

*"But now ask the beasts and let them teach you. And
the birds of the heavens and let them tell you"*

Job 12:7
(NIV)

The Last Wish

The last wish of old Bill Hayward was one he hoped would come true
And that was to see his beloved donkeys, Maggie, Trilby and Boo
To see and touch them once again, would make his day just great
To whisper their names as he rubbed their ears, to say goodbye to his mates

The look on his face was priceless, as we led them to the lawn
Where old Bill was sitting with family and friends, reminiscing of times long gone
He struggled to rise from his hospital chair, a bit unsteady on his feet
And a smile broke out on his pale lined face that caused us all to weep

'Oh Trilby!' Bill said "my old mate! and Maggie! and how ya goin' Boo?
It seems so long since I left home and I've been missing you
I didn't want to leave you, but the doctors said I must
It's the end of the road my old mates, I'm full of asbestos dust"

He cupped their faces and stroked their necks, as quietly they stood
And fed them carrots and some bread as equally as he could
There was a bond between them, you could see it plain as day
And it made us all both happy and sad to see them together this way

"I've had a great life" Bill said to me, "I'm grateful for the life that I've had
With Robyn my wife and my kids by my side, we were happy in good times and bad
I've tried to help others and do what's right for my family, my work and my friends
And I'm so glad to see them today, as I've come to my journey's end

Some stories were told of the Bill Hayward of old, nicknamed "skinny" as a kid
How he rode the wild horses, fished, shot kangaroos - he was good at whatever he did
A man with a quiet manner, successful and determined - but don't get in his way
They claimed he was just like Clint Eastwood, cross him and make his day

"I've always loved the horses, he said, I started droving when I turned fifteen
Then worked on outback stations oh! the places that I've seen
I changed it all for the love of my life and work with the airlines out west
And I could see he was satisfied with all he'd done, because he knew he'd done his best

"yes, I've always loved the horses, but the donkeys are simply great
Over the last four years I'd get up early and they'd be waiting at the gate
They'd come to me and fill my life with love and lots of laughter
It makes me happy to see them again and I know they'll be looked after"

Tears filled his eyes as he looked all around to see his loved ones had all come
To say what's on their hearts and minds before God takes him home
I caught a glimpse of the man he was, genuine through and through
That's why granting his last wish, was a wonderful thing to do.

Prayer

Heavenly Father, Almighty God.

*I thank you God and praise you, for making a way, when
there was no way; for keeping Bill Hayward alive long
enough to be reunited with his beloved animals.*

He thought he would never see them again.

*But you are a God of great compassion and we are grateful for the opportunity
you gave us, to bring a little joy to a dying man. All those present felt your
presence. All those present witnessed the love flow between Bill and his pets.*

*Maggie, Trilby and Boo knew him. They crowded around
him and did not wander from his side.*

*Whether they sensed his sadness, or not, I don't know, but they would not leave
him and he couldn't bear to tear himself away from them even though his
strength was failing. He called for help to stand up so that he could still keep
touching the faces, rubbing the ears, breathing deeply their donkey scent. It
was a precious moment Lord, to see Bill drinking in that special fragrance.*

*We all knew that he knew he would be leaving soon and he wanted to take his
friends with him but this was all he could take – the memories, the love and joy.*

*Father God, Holy Trinity, by giving Bill this moment, you gave Bill peace
and permission to go. You are a loving God, one like no other and I thank
you and praise you Lord for your love and kindness to old Bill Hayward*

Is it crazy to praise God for a fallen world?

It seems crazy but no! A fallen world brings us back to the reason we need God in our lives. A fallen world means people have moved away from God and live for themselves. A fallen world is what we make it. It's us, thinking we know better than God, making it up as we go and living through our feelings. There's a lack of knowledge about who God is. People confuse religion with Christianity and reject God.

In today's world you can see it. The decline of Christianity is closely related to the rise of violence, hatred, rebellion, confusion, intolerance, selfishness. We've lost our moral compass.

A fallen world means we need God more than ever. Have you ever felt the peace of God? To feel that all is right with the world, even though your rational mind says there are so many things wrong with the world, but you don't get frightened by that. You have an inner peace, a calmness, even joy sometimes, knowing God's got your back and everything is good and you will be ok. That is such freedom.

In Christ we have a firm foundation on which to live and create a peaceful world.

A better world is what God makes through us. We learn through His Word how to live beyond ourselves and live for others. It's crazy but it works and I praise God for His Word about self-control, love, patience, empathy and all the other ways we teaches.

We need to pray that the removal of the Word of God from our society is reversed. We need to bring God back, not take Him out.

"These things I have spoken to you, that in Me you may
have peace. In the world you will have tribulation; but
be of good cheer, I have overcome the world"

John 16:33
(NIV)

What Would Life be Without God?

What would life be without God? You have only to look and see
The chaos that surrounds our lives, the decline of our society
The rebellion, the anger, the violence and lies
The hopelessness, the wickedness, the increasing suicides

We think we're so progressive, so modern in our ways
We accept the latest "thing" because it's the latest craze
We've lost things to believe in, things that were a solid foundation
We're taught to question everything, and everyone, in every situation

No trust in authority, no belief in anything
Satan knows he's on a winner, to undermine our faith and feeling
Its so hard now to speak the truth, no-one wants to hear
Each person's truth is their reality, however that appears

What was once considered unacceptable is now just commonplace
Self-respect has vanished and left no visible trace
Everyone tries to make their mark with their freedom of expression
Forgetting it's your character, that makes the best impression

I feel sorry for the children, bombarded with all sorts of things
That rob them of their childhood and all the confusion that it brings
Families find it hard to stay together, they only talk by mobile phone
Though they all live in the family house, it doesn't feel like home

Time is racing, life is hectic, there's no chance to stop a while
Take a look at peoples' faces, it's hard to find a smile
It seems we've lost the joy of life – we need to get our lives on track
Life without God is a little bit threatening, we need to bring Him back!

Is it crazy to praise God for natural disasters?

for the bushfires, floods and drought that wreck such havoc on our environment and communities? You would think it crazy if you only saw the disaster, but I praise God for what happens afterwards. The help that comes from the community, from churches, from neighbours. We see God in action more, in the aftermath of disaster, than we see at any other time. I thank Him for the compassionate heart He has put in people and for the help those people give.

My husband and I received such a blessing from our Church community after the floods in February. We live in the hinterland on the Sunshine Coast, on a horse property bordered by the Mary River. In twenty-two years we had never seen so much water, that ran so swiftly and violently. We thought we were safe, but we weren't. The shock of that and of seeing the debris and damage afterwards, had a devastating effect on me. I was overwhelmed by the task ahead of us, to clean up, to get horses back into their paddocks and to try to return our lives to normal.

I prayed for help and God answered my prayer. He sent a team of 25 people, volunteers from our Church to come and clean up. My God is merciful and kind and there is a lesson in this for all of us. Never think, for a moment, that you have to fight your battles alone. God is always with us and He never gives us a burden more than we can bear.

> *"So do not fear, for I am with you;*
> *do not be dismayed, for I am your God.*
> *I will strengthen you and help you;*
> *I will uphold you with my righteous right hand."*

> Isaiah 41:10
> (NIV)

Last Thursday

When people ask me where is God? I can honestly say
I've seen Him and I know He's real, He was at our farm, last Thursday
He turned up with a chainsaw, a shovel and a rake
To help clean up and return the joy, that Satan tried to take

He turned up with a whippersnapper, gumboots and a hat
A Polaris, quad bike, wheelbarrows and trailers – we didn't expect all that
He turned up in the Women of Worth, whose very presence eased our pain
they supported the team, pruned and cleaned, the world feels right again

God came in the smiles and handshakes and hugs that said don't worry, we'll get
    this done
We're here for you and we'll help you through, your battle till it's won
We know its personal, you feel under attack, nothing seems to be going right
You've been knocked down but we'll help you up, we're with you in this fight

God and His angels set to work and worked right through the day
Backs bent to the task of clearing, the flood debris away
It was a perfect day for working, blue sky and soft gentle breeze
My husband slashing fence lines and moving fallen trees

For each section cleared, it was symbolic, like a darkness lifting from our hearts
The flooding had left such a huge mess, we were overwhelmed by the task
God in His great love, sent our church community to help us refresh and renew
They volunteered to come and help and see what they could do

I don't know why bad things happen, but out of it comes the good
God has His way of teaching us, in a way that's understood
Life's trials and tempests come to test us, sometimes it's hard to endure
When everything seems against us, but of one thing I am sure

No matter what we suffer, God will help us find a way
Like He did by sending the people from Church on the Rise Maleny, who came out
    to help last Thursday
Faith with works is a blessing, that's what God wants us to do, is what we Christians
    understand
I pray that God will bless them as they blessed us, with their hearts and hands.

Have you ever seen God in action like this? The swarms of volunteers who want to help? It is such a blessing for you and for them. There are many Christian communities, some set up specifically to step in following a disaster and others just arise, as in our case. When our church heard of what happened it was spontaneous – a phone call – we're coming to help what's a good day? We don't know how many will come, but we're coming. If you hurt, we hurt too. And there it was, all organised and on the day 25 people came to help. I cried when I saw them all and how eagerly and energetically they set to the huge task ahead of them.

God blessed us with a perfect day, sunny but not too hot, a summer breeze but not too strong. I remember looking to the heavens to thank God for this moment and I saw the most beautiful and endless blue sky, not a cloud to be seen. I became aware of the trees and the birds, the snort of a horse, a dog barking in the distance, voices being carried on the wind. In that moment I felt my anxiety melt away and knew that God was in control. Although our world had been turned upside down, He would make it right again.

Two weeks earlier, when the floodwaters rose so swiftly, my husband and I had to rescue horses from the big paddock. In fifteen minutes the water rose from knee height, to waist height, to chest height as I led our horses from the paddock to higher ground. My faithful dog was with me and she was being swept away by the current. I just managed to grab her collar and hang on until we came out of the water. It was a terrifying experience and I thank God that He was looking out for us and kept us safe in that dangerous situation.

Have you experienced God in your life in a similar situation? Write down the times He has come to your rescue.

Prayer

*Heavenly Father, I praise You and thank You for watching over us
and keeping us safe in the floods. I praise you and thank you, for
your mercy and your kindness and for answering our prayers.*

*I praise you and thank you, that you saw how despairing we were as we
looked at the devastation and debris once the waters subsided. You knew
exactly what we needed and you put it into the hearts of our church
community to spend a day with us, helping us and lifting our spirits.
We praise you and thank you for keeping everyone safe as they worked
energetically with chainsaws and power tools to get the job done.*

Lord, our property is restored.

Our hearts are filled with gratitude and hope lives in us again.

*Father God, I pray that you will bless each and every person for
the blessing they bestowed on us. I pray that through the poem
I wrote to honour them, people will see You in action.*

Amen

"Of all the commandments, which is the most important?'

*The most important one, answered Jesus is this: "Hear O Israel; the Lord
our God, the Lord is one. Love the Lord your God with all your heart and
with all your soul and with all your mind and with all your strength.'*

*The second is this: "Love your neighbour as yourself.
There is no commandment greater than these"*

Mark 12:28-31
(NIV)

Sometimes it's hard to praise God for our busy lives. When we're so weighed down with responsibility, too much work and not enough time or we simply don't have the strength, or the will, to keep going like we used to. We've lost our joy and it's just work, work, work, same old, same old story.

Or, we're so wound up with a situation that it's affecting our health. We can't sleep, we're not eating properly, we shed frustrated and angry tears, We need answers and can't find any. No-one really understands why we are so stressed out about it.

Is it crazy to pick that time to praise God? No! that's when you should praise Him harder.

God has an answer. Be still

"The Lord will fight for you; you need only to be still"

Exodus 14:14
(NIV)

He says, "Be still and know that I am God; I will be exalted among the nations, I will be exalted in the earth"

Psalms 46:10
(NIV)

Be Still

When your life is filled with busyness, there's so many things to do
You're driven to get things done, people rely on you
The days become a blur, the night offers little relief
It's got to end sometime soon, that's a hope more than belief
Be still

When your mind's in constant turmoil, going over the same old ground
Seeking answers to your questions, but answers can't be found
When overthinking, overreaction, overstating the situation
Just heightens your anxiety and adds to your frustration
Be still

When the demands are overwhelming and you have nowhere left to turn
When you find your joy is stolen and all your bridges burned
When you know deep down inside yourself, that something's just not right
But you can't seem to stop yourself, from being so uptight
Be still

Be still and wait upon the Lord, He'll lighten your heavy load
Be still and wait upon the Lord, He'll guide you down a better road
Be still and wait upon the Lord, He'll take your stress away
And bring you peace and joy and love and bring them back to stay
Be still

These things He can do, if you believe He can
These things He will do, if you believe in His plan
Two simple words that seem impossible to do
But with God all things are possible, the choice to do it, is up to you
Be still

Make a decision to wake earlier, to start off each new day
Reading and studying the Bible and having time just to pray
Memorise scripture and keep it fixed in your mind
To calm your anxiety – it works every time
Be still

Each day look for beauty, like a sunset, slowly fading over the hill
You don't have to be stopped, for your heart to be still
God hears you whisper, thank you Lord for this day
He's ready to answer, just follow His ways
Be still

Be still is the secret, it doesn't take long
To find rest for your stress and lift your heart with a song
Be still is the answer we have to accept
Be still is the solution you'll never regret
Be still

Prayer

My Lord and Saviour, I praise you for the many ways you talk to me. Sometimes you have to do it with a mighty roar because I'm just not listening. I'm too busy, or too anxious and you have to get my attention.

Sometimes it's a piece of Scripture or worship song that repeats and repeats in my head, until I'm forced to stop and think about it; and sometimes, it's that still small voice that gently reminds me to be still and wait for You.

Lord, when you speak to me like that, it calms my busy mind. I breathe deeply and allow myself to relax, preparing to welcome you into my mind and heart.

You are a wise God. One who knows much more than we will ever know. You know Lord, that Be Still is a powerful weapon against spiritual attack. It seems such a passive thing, but when practiced, it steels and strengthens us, as we meditate and contemplate Your Word and Scripture.

You are a loving God, who leads us from the path of self-destruction through your whispered Be Still. It is so easy to be tricked into busyness and use this as a distraction from having to deal with whatever we need to deal with, our problems never solved, solutions never found, wounds never healed. But You Lord, know this and because You love us, You whisper to us Be Still.

Lord, let me always hear your whisper and respond to your command.

Amen

Is it crazy to praise God for old age? For the aching bones, the tiredness, the relentless nothingness of days? You've got stories to tell but no-one to tell them to. Praise God you've lived a life. Many people don't get to old age so praise God for every day you are still here.

Is it crazy to praise God for your job that carries a heavy load of authority and responsibility? Every decision you make is criticized, scrutinized, challenged and you're tired but you must go on. Praise God you've got a job and purpose – many people have neither, so praise God for the good things in your life.

Is it crazy to praise God for being poor and the worry and struggle that goes with trying to make ends meet, particularly when you have a family to support? You've got two jobs and you're doing the best that you can but the bills keep coming. You just wonder where it will all end. Praise God and ask Him to give you the strength to hang on till better times come. The sacrifice you make is love in action. Your children see it, your friends see it and Praise God your spouse will love you for it.

Is it crazy to praise God for all our anxieties, doubts, questions about your own worth, about your place in the world, about your relationships? Praise God that He is there waiting for you, to help you, to calm you, to revive you and to show you how to live the better life.

"Come to me all you who are weary and burdened and I will give you rest. Take my yoke upon you and learn from me, for I am gentle and humble in heart and you will find rest for your souls. For my yoke is easy and my burden is light"

Matthew 11:28-30
(NIV)

Come to Me All who are weary

Jesus knows what it's like to be weary, to be so burdened down
So overwhelmed with sorrow, as when He wore that thorny crown
His suffering on that road to Calvary, his death and cruel end
Jesus knows what it's like to be weary, He's our Saviour and our friend

He is God and became a man, to feel our pain and limitations
As God He had no constraints, but as a man .. tried his endurance and His patience
He came to save the lost and lonely, the poor and meek, the ones in chains
And he showed us what real love is, He died so we could live, again

Jesus knows what it's like to be weighed down, to carry a burden that's his alone
In the garden in Gethsemine, he cried take this burden from me, not my will but
        yours be done
And so it is when we reach our limits, when we beg and cry out for some relief
Jesus hears and beckons us forward, till we find his grace and peace

We can rest there in His promise, where all our troubles melt away
And for a moment, or for a lifetime, we can hear Him say
'Take my yoke and learn from me, I am gentle and humble in heart
Learn my ways and lean on me, your road's been long but the end's not far'

Listen to His quiet whisper "you believed in me and it's got you through
I know you are still troubled, so for now, I will carry you
I'm here for you child, take my yoke upon you, it's easy and my burden is light
With me in your life you'll be so much stronger, I can make all things right"

Come to me all who are weary, lay your burdens down
Come and rest and let me help you, I can turn your life around
Turn your sorrow into gladness, bring your troubles to the Lord
Come and find the peace He offers, the peace that's found only in God's Word

NOTES:

Write down the many ways you can think of where you can praise God

Closing Prayer

Lord, I thank you for your inspired words. I pray they touch the hearts of all who read this book and that each person finds a message just for them.

Lord, I thank you for the power of words – words that can help and heal, words that will open minds to understanding and provide insight on a personal level.

I pray that faith will be strengthened for believers and faith will be ignited for non-believers who find this book in their hands. It's meant to be there.

God is merciful, kind and powerful. His love is faithful and eternal. We just have to believe in Him to receive His blessings.

Praise Him, Almighty God

Amen

About the Author

Chris Bourne is an author, poet, performer and lyricist. Writing has always been a part of her life but since retiring to the Sunshine Coast in 2015, Christine has published three books, two audio books, written a worship song "Goliath" which featured on her audio book "Who is Your Goliath" and has performed her poetry about life and Christian poetry in venues across the Sunshine Coast. "Crazy Praises" is her third book of contemporary Christian poetry and she has another three books underway. Retirement does not mean rest for this busy woman.

Christine has also discovered the capacity of social media and has a Facebook site where she produced two series of extracts from her father's memoir "The Last Mile" as podcasts.

Life is busy as Chris juggles her writing along with serving as Secretary for Maleny High School Chaplaincy, regularly attending Church on the Rise Maleny and the Women on the Rise group, attending St Margaret's Anglican at Woombye, helping her husband run their horse property and doing some pastoral care using her Diploma of Christian Counselling in a practical way. Bible reading and study is an integral part of her daily morning routine and finds her daily reading gives her insight and ideas for more Christian poems.

The great loves of her life are God, her family, her church families, her horses Nugget and Buddy, her dog Joy and living the country life.

For more copies of this book for yourself or as a gift, you can contact Christine by:

Web: www.christinejbourneauthor.com.au
Facebook: ChristineJbourneauthor
Email: Christinejbourneauthor@gmail.com
Phone: 0428 176 557

www.ingramcontent.com/pod-product-compliance
Lightning Source LLC
Chambersburg PA
CBHW062025040426
42447CB00010B/2138